OTHER WAYS TO SAY

300 synonyms
for 50 common words

Karen Kovacs

Learn English with Karen

Learn English with Karen

Other Ways to Say: 300 synonyms for 50 common words
Text © Karen Kovacs, 2023
Logo © Karen Kovacs, 2023

No part of this book may be reproduced, scanned or distributed in any printed or electronic form without permission. Please do not participate in or encourage piracy of copyrighted materials in violation of the author's rights. Thank you for respecting the hard work of the author.

More books by the same author to improve your English fast

I also write **graded readers**. These are exciting stories that are **adapted to your level**. There are **definitions** of difficult words at the back. Learn **without any extra studying**.

Studies show that learners who read a lot in English **improve in all areas** much more **quickly** than learners who don't read.

www.ReadStories-LearnEnglish.com

If you want to improve your IELTS score, this is the book for you. It has practice exam questions, pronunciation exercises, exam tips, model answers & more. More info on my website.

CONTENTS

Introduction Page 6

Unit 1 Very good
 2 Very bad
 3 Very big
 4 Very small
 5 Attractive
 6 Ugly
 7 Easy
 8 Difficult
 9 Happy
 10 Sad
 11 Heavy
 12 Light
 13 Dark
 14 Bright
 15 Intelligent
 16 Stupid
 17 I love
 18 I don't like
 19 Interesting
 20 Boring
 21 Clean
 22 Dirty
 23 Have a good relationship
 24 Have a bad relationship
 25 Close
 26 Far

27	Thirsty
28	Hungry
29	Expensive
30	Cheap
31	Eat
32	Speak
33	Wait
34	Look
35	Walk
36	Sleep
37	Die
38	Surprised
39	Tired
40	Lucky
41	Funny
42	Busy
43	Job
44	A lot
45	Important
46	Hello
47	Bye
48	Thank you
49	I'm sorry
50	I think

Answers	Page 108
Get a free story	Page 121

Introduction

Why do you need this book?

Often, when we speak, we rely on the same words again and again.

Good, very good ... quite interesting, not very interesting ...

This isn't always a problem and native speakers sometimes use simple words too. But to improve your comprehension and fluency, you need to increase your vocabulary .... and if you're taking an exam in English, then you must have a wide range of vocabulary to impress the examiner and get a good mark!

This book will really increase your confidence in English. And it includes not only words but whole phrases too, which is a fantastic way to take your English to the next level.

Who is this book for?

This book is ideal for students at intermediate level (B1) and above, for self-study or classroom use.

It is for students who want to learn general English. The focus of this book is *not* on academic or business English. Most of the vocabulary is informal or neutral, with a few formal words and phrases too.

If you're a teacher, then this book would be great to use in your classes to improve your students' grasp of English. They can also have fun with the vocabulary as many of the words and phrases are interesting and very expressive!

What dialect is this book written in?

The book contains vocabulary that any native British English speaker will understand. The dialect is best described as standard British English and the book does *not* include other regional or international varieties.

I have made sure that all the vocabulary in this book is current and useful.

Who am I?

My name is Karen Kovacs. I was born in the UK and I still live here.

I have a master's degree in linguistics and a diploma in the teaching of English as a Foreign Language. I'm the author of a large number of books. Look on my website for details of my other books:

www.ReadStories-LearnEnglish.com

I have taught English in the UK and abroad, and I speak three foreign languages (Hungarian, French and Spanish). This gives me a deep understanding of what it's like to learn a language and of what learners most need to learn.

Notes on using this book

- Not all the words and phrases are exact synonyms. Some are different parts of speech, some are more/less formal and some have slightly different usages. I've left notes in brackets after the words to help you.
- If a word is informal or formal, I have included that after the word in brackets. If you see nothing (neither *formal* nor *informal*), then the word is neutral.
- Pay attention to the example sentences to see how the word is used in context.
- Language is complex and some synonyms don't work in exactly the same way as the original word. Check online or in a dictionary for more detailed guidance on usage for a specific word or phrase if you need to.
- Of course, there are other synonyms that aren't included in this book – I can't include every synonym in English.

The practice exercises

- There are practice exercises for every section of this book. You don't have to do them but they will help you remember the vocabulary.
- You might need to cover the vocabulary or cover the first page of exercises, so that you can't cheat!
- The answers are at the back of the book.

1 Very good

amazing

*I recommend this book – it is absolutely **amazing**.*

something else

(informal)

*The view from this room really is **something else**. You can see all the way to the sea.*

in a class of its own

*These musicians are **in a class of their own**. Nobody can play like them.*

brilliant

*The party was **brilliant**. I didn't want to leave.*

first-rate

*The food here is **first-rate**. I wish I could eat here every day.*

outstanding

(a little formal)

*That film was truly **outstanding**. The special effects were so convincing and the actors top-notch.*

2 Very bad

horrendous

He suffered **horrendous** injuries and will have to remain in hospital for a long time.

awful

Look, the weather's **awful** so we can't go for a walk after all, I'm afraid.

terrible

I have some **terrible** news. You'd better sit down.

the pits

(informal)

This place is **the pits**. Why did we come here on holiday?

not up to scratch

I know I'm my own worst critic but my performance today was just **not up to scratch**.

second-rate

This play is so **second-rate**. Will anything exciting happen at all?

Very good, very bad

a. Without looking back at the vocabulary pages, put the following words and phrases in the correct columns.

amazing	awful	brilliant
first-rate	horrendous	in a class of its own
not up to scratch	outstanding	second-rate
something else	terrible	the pits

Very good	Very bad
1.	1.
2.	2.
3.	3.
4.	4.
5.	5.
6.	6.

b. Complete the sentences with a word or phrase meaning *very good* or *very bad*. The first letter of each word is given.

1. We had an a_____ time at Will and Jen's house. I wish you could have been there.

2. This hotel is f_____-r_____. We must leave them a positive review.

3. My English class is t_____ p_____. They keep interrupting the teacher and I'm not learning anything.

4. I'm sorry but the service we've received here is simply n_____ u_____ t_____ s_____.

5. Sorry I'm late. The traffic was h_____.

6. Harry is i_____ a c_____ o_____ h_____ o_____. He's so good that nobody can compete with him.

7. The painting is an o_____ example of early Impressionist art.

8. What t_____ music! Turn it off!

9. They had an a_____ time at the racecourse. I don't think they'll ever go again.

10. They're such a s_____-r_____ football team. I don't know why he still supports them.

3 Very big

huge

*That dog is **huge**. I'm a bit scared of it, to be honest.*

as big as a house

(informal, funny, physically big/overweight)

*I don't like myself in this outfit. I look **as big as a house**.*

whopping great

(informal, only used before a noun)

*She's got a **whopping great** bruise on her arm from when she fell.*

massive

*Are you going to eat the whole cake? It's **massive**!*

immense

*This machine uses **immense** amounts of energy.*

gigantic

*A **gigantic** tree had fallen across the road so we couldn't get through.*

4 Very small

miniscule

*I've only got a week to finish this project. That's a **miniscule** amount of time.*

fit in the palm of your hand

*The baby tortoise was so small it could **fit in the palm of my hand**.*

tiny

*This room is **tiny**! How can we fit our double bed in here?*

microscopic

(informal)

*I'm not going to that restaurant again. Their portion sizes are **microscopic**.*

invisible to the naked eye

Bacteria are **invisible to the naked eye**.

minute

*The photo shows you the inside of the flower in **minute** detail.*

Very big, very small

a. Do these words and phrases mean *very big* or *very small*? Put a tick ✓ in the correct column.

	Very big	Very small
1. miniscule		
2. fit in the palm of your hand		
3. whopping great		
4. massive		
5. tiny		
6. huge		
7. as big as a house		
8. microscopic		
9. gigantic		
10. invisible to the naked eye		
11. minute		
12. immense		

b. Complete the sentences using a suitable word or phrase. There is more than one possible answer.

1. Buckingham Palace is _____.

2. I barely saw the mouse. It was _____.

3. Look at that _____ tree! It must be really old.

4. Germs are _____.

5. Your bedroom is _____. How will you be able to fit a double bed in it?

6. That elephant is _____. I'm glad it's behind bars!

7. It's not fair. Your present is much bigger than mine. Mine is _____.

5 Attractive

easy on the eye
(informal, funny)
He's a model so he's very **easy on the eye**.

drop-dead gorgeous
(very attractive, informal)
She's **drop-dead gorgeous**, there's no doubt about it.

hot
(informal)
He thinks he's **hot** but arrogance isn't attractive, is it?

fanciable
She's been voted the world's most **fanciable** woman for the second year running.

fit
(informal)
This actor is **fit**. Has he been in any other films?

exquisite
(formal, usually used about an object)
What an **exquisite** painting!

6 Ugly

minger

(informal)

You shouldn't say she's a **minger** – that's rude.

not much to look at

(informal)

I'm **not much to look at** but I've got a great personality!

no oil painting

(informal, funny)

He's **no oil painting** but I love him. He's so kind to me.

hideous

(very ugly)

You can't wear that purple suit. It's absolutely **hideous** and you know it!

unprepossessing

(formal)

What an **unprepossessing** house. Why don't they knock it down?

unsightly

(a little formal)

That graffiti is so **unsightly**. I wish they'd paint over it.

Attractive, ugly

a. Complete the words and phrases meaning *attractive*. The first letter of each word is given.

1. e_____ on the e_____

2. e_____

3. h_____

4. d_____-d_____ g_____

5. f_____

6. f_____

b. Complete the words and phrases meaning *ugly*. The first letter of each word is given.

1. not m_____ to l_____ at

2. u_____

3. u_____

4. no o_____ p_____

5. m_____

6. h_____

c. Think of a different famous person for each question.

1. someone who is not much to look at

   _____

2. someone you think is fanciable

   _____

3. someone drop-dead gorgeous

   _____

4. someone who is is no oil painting

   _____

5. someone you find hot

   _____

d. Name something you have seen that is ...

1. unprepossessing.

2. unsightly.

3. exquisite.

7 Easy

walk in the park

(informal)

He's used to long bikes rides, so this will be a **walk in the park** for him.

piece of cake

(very easy, informal)

Try it! Honestly, it's **a piece of cake**.

foolproof

(used about a method, plan, machine etc)

The instructions are completely **foolproof** so you won't have any problems.

breeze

(informal, very easy to achieve)

Learning English is a **breeze**.

can do it in your sleep

(very easy, informal)

I've walked there so many times I **could do it in my sleep**.

not rocket science

(informal)

Come on, it's **not rocket science**! Just mix all the ingredients together.

8 Difficult

tricky

*This question is **tricky**. Shall I give up and go onto the next one?*

no picnic

(informal)

*Looking after young children is **no picnic**, I can tell you.*

demanding

*It's a **demanding** job but I get a lot of job satisfaction.*

hard-pressed to

(find something difficult)

*You'd be **hard-pressed to** find a better chef than him.*

arduous

(a little formal)

*This task is more **arduous** than I expected.*

taxing

(a little formal)

*We won't ask you to do anything too **taxing**, don't worry.*

Easy, difficult

a. Rearrange the words in the large letters. The words, or the phrases they are part of, all mean *easy*.

1. I can do it in my lespe. It really isn't hard.

2. It's a walk in the rpka. Don't make such a big deal of it.

3. It's not otkrce science. Just think for a minute.

4. Learning languages is a eiepc of cake.

5. What are you talking about? Baking is a rbzeee. You just have to follow the recipe.

6. Stop hesitating! Our plan is 100% rflopfoo.

b. Rearrange the words in the large letters. The words, or the phrases they are part of, all mean *difficult*.

1. What an srauodu journey. I'm glad it's over now.

2. My career is quite xtgain but I do enjoy it.

3. Feeding yourself on a tight budget is no cpcnii.

4. I'm hard-pdsseer to find anything wrong with this book.

5. Learning a language can be kytcri at first but don't give up.

6. My schedule is very manedngdi at the moment.

c. Delete one word or phrase so that each sentence is true for you. Explain your answers.

1. For me, learning English is **a piece of cake / no picnic**.

2. My job is **arduous / a breeze**.

3. I have a **good / bad** sense of direction. Finding my way around is **a walk in the park / tricky** for me.

4. DIY is **not rocket science / really taxing**. I **never / sometimes / always** call in a professional.

9 Happy

jump for joy

(very happy)

If I pass my exam, I'm going to be **jumping for joy**.

thrilled

(very happy)

I was absolutely **thrilled** to hear your good news.

chuffed

(informal)

I'm well **chuffed** – I've just found out that I'm getting a pay rise.

glad

I'm so **glad** you're feeling better at last.

smile from ear to ear

(look happy)

Look at her – she's **smiling from ear to ear**.

over the moon

(very happy, informal)

Our first grandchild has just been born. We're **over the moon**.

10 Sad

down

(informal)

He's been really **down** since his girlfriend dumped him.

depressed

(very sad)

I feel **depressed** – I'm going to watch a good comedy to cheer myself up.

cut up

(informal)

Lucy and Tom have split up and she's pretty **cut up** about it.

grief-stricken

(very sad, a little formal)

I'm utterly **grief-stricken**. My favourite actor has died.

reduced to tears

(formal)

I was **reduced to tears** by her constant criticisms.

downcast

(formal)

Why do you look so **downcast**? The sun is shining.

Happy, sad

a. Matches the words to make phrases. They all mean *happy* or *sad*.

1. smile from ...   a. joy
2. over the ...   b. stricken
3. grief-...   c. tears
4. reduced to ...   d. up
5. jump for ...   e. moon
6. cut ...   f. ear to ear

b. In the last task, which phrases mean *happy* and which mean *sad*?

c. Can you remember the words that mean *sad*?

1. d_____

2. d_____

3. d_____

d. How about the words that mean *happy*?

1. t_____

2. g_____

3. c_____

e. Complete the sentences about things that make *you* happy or sad.

1. I'm always chuffed when _____

2. When _____, I smiled ear to ear.

3. I was so cut up when _____

4. I was thrilled when _____

5. I feel a bit depressed when _____

6. When _____, I jumped for joy.

11 Heavy

weigh a tonne

(very heavy, informal)

*This bag **weighs a tonne**. What on earth do you have in here?*

dead weight

(heavy and difficult to carry)

*Her body went limp and she was a **dead weight**.*

hefty

(large and heavy)

*He's a pretty **hefty** bloke, you've got to admit.*

laden

(carrying something heavy)

*The trees are **laden** with fruit.*

weighty

*It's a **weighty** box so be careful when you lift it.*

top-heavy

(heavier at the top so not well balanced)

*The boat only capsized because it was **top-heavy**.*

12 Light

light as a feather
(very light)
I can easily pick her up. She's as **light as a feather**.

not weigh a thing
(very light, informal)
It's alright, thanks. I don't need help. This **doesn't weigh a thing**.

insubstantial
(lacking solidity)
These tents are pretty **insubstantial**. Will we be ok in the storm?

weigh nothing
(very light, informal)
Can you take this suitcase too? Don't worry, it **weighs nothing**.

lightweight
Laptops are more **lightweight** than they were a few years ago.

portable
(light enough to be carried)
Luckily the medical equipment is fully **portable**.

Heavy, light

a. Put the following words and phrases in the correct column.

dead weight	hefty	insubstantial
laden	light as a feather	lightweight
not weigh a thing	portable	top-heavy
weigh a tonne	weigh nothing	weighty

Heavy	Light
1.	1.
2.	2.
3.	3.
4.	4.
5.	5.
6.	6.

b. In each sentence, underline the correct word or phrase in bold.

1. I picked her up really easily. She was **as light as a feather / top-heavy**.

2. Early aeroplanes were fairly **insubstantial / weighty** – they were just made of wood.

3. This bag weighs **nothing / a tonne**. Can you help carry it up the stairs?

4. I came home **lightweight / laden** with heavy boxes.

5. She was asleep so her body was **a dead weight / portable** and difficult to carry.

13 Dark

gloomy

(dark and also scary or sad)

*What a **gloomy** old house. Who lives there, do you think?*

murky

(dark and difficult to see through)

*The glass is really **murky**. I can't see what's inside.*

poorly lit

(used about a room with very little light)

*The room was so **poorly lit** that I couldn't see what I was eating!*

pitch-black

(completely dark)

*The stage was **pitch-black**, but then they turned on a spotlight.*

dim

(used about lights that aren't bright)

*The streetlights here are far too **dim**. I wish they were brighter.*

can't see a thing

(very dark, informal)

*Turn on the torch on your phone. I **can't see a thing**.*

14 Bright

dazzling

(so bright you're unable to see for a moment)

*Look at his **dazzling** white teeth. He's had them whitened.*

glaring

(so bright that it is uncomfortable)

*Can you please turn down that **glaring** light? It's giving me a headache.*

Day-Glo™

(used for orange, yellow, pink, green)

*He was wearing a **Day-Glo** jumper, which looked really cool.*

gleaming

(bright and clean)

*After she'd finished, the kitchen was **gleaming**!*

loud

(too bright and not showing good taste)

*He wore a **loud**, patterned shirt. It looked terrible.*

ablaze with

(a little formal)

*The trees in autumn are **ablaze with** colour.*

Dark, bright

a. Complete the antonym (opposite) of each word.

1. dim   g_____
2. murky   g_____
3. gloomy   d_____

b. Complete the sentences with the appropriate word.

1. She bought a T-shirt in a _____-Glo orange colour. I would have gone for a paler colour, personally.

2. The exam hall was so _____ lit that I struggled to read the questions on the paper.

3. In spring, the garden is _____ with colour.

4. Why have you turned the lights off? I can't see a _____.

c. Answer the questions.

1. When did you last see something that was ablaze with colour?

_____

2. Do you own any loud shirts or T-shirts? How do you feel when you wear them?

_____

3. Can you only sleep if the room is pitch-black?

_____

4. Do you dislike gloomy weather?

_____

15 Intelligent

not just a pretty face

(informal, funny)

You didn't know I could play the piano? Ah, I'm **not just a pretty face!**

clever

I'd like to be a vet but there's no way I'm **clever** enough.

bright

He's naturally **bright** but he's lazy, I'm afraid.

brainbox

(very intelligent, informal)

You're such a **brainbox**! You always know all the answers.

bright spark

(informal)

She's such a **bright spark**. She's at the top of her class.

learned

(formal, someone who has studied a lot)

He's ever so **learned**. He works at the university.

16 Stupid

thick

(informal)

*Stop being so **thick**! Surely you know the answer!*

brain-dead

(very stupid, informal)

*You'd have to be completely **brain-dead** to pay such a lot of money for a car.*

dumb

*You told him your password? That was a **dumb** thing to do.*

slow

*He's a bit **slow**, isn't he? Why doesn't he understand?*

clueless

(not knowing about a particular thing)

*She's utterly **clueless** about computers so don't ask her.*

slow-witted

(formal)

*The **slow-witted** interviewer asked all the wrong questions.*

Intelligent, stupid

a. Are the words in bold adjectives or nouns?

1. What a bright **spark** you are. Well done for getting that right.

2. People say he's a **brainbox** but he failed his last exam.

3. Are you **dumb**? I've told you a thousand times that I'm allergic to nuts.

4. Sorry, I'm being **thick**. Can you explain it again?

5. I don't know how he can be president when he is that **slow-witted**.

b. Read the sentence. Then write four sentences with the same meaning, using the words below.

You have to admit, she's very intelligent.

1. not just a pretty face

_____

2. bright

_____

3. brainbox

_____

4. bright spark

_____

c. Make a list of ten famous people.

1. _____   6. _____
2. _____   7. _____
3. _____   8. _____
4. _____   9. _____
5. _____   10. _____

d. Now make a sentence for each person, using a word or phrase to describe whether they are intelligent or stupid.

1. _____
2. _____
3. _____
4. _____
5. _____
6. _____
7. _____
8. _____
9. _____
10. _____

17 I love

right up my street

(informal)

*Thanks for the film recommendation. I loved it – it was **right up my street**.*

really into

(informal)

*I'm **really into** fantasy books. I read nothing else.*

live for

*I **live for** football. I watch all the matches on the TV and I play it too.*

keen on

*They're quite **keen on** cooking and they're getting better every day.*

adore

*I **adore** singing. I should probably join a choir.*

have a lot of time for

(informal, used about a person)

*I **have a lot of time for** Adam. He's a good friend – very kind and thoughtful.*

18 I don't like

not my cup of tea

(informal)

Hip-hop music just **isn't my cup of tea**.

not my thing

(informal)

Dancing is **not my thing**, I have to admit.

not crazy about

(informal)

I'm **not crazy about** that film.

more of a ... person

(informal)

I don't like him. I'm **more of a** Johnny Depp **person**.

can't stand

(really dislike)

I **can't stand** ice-cream. It makes my teeth hurt!

not fond of

(a little formal)

I'm **not fond of** dogs. In my family, we've always had cats.

I love, I don't like

a. Complete the sentences with the correct word.

1. I _____ for music. I'm in a band and I write my own songs as well.

2. He's OK but I'm more of a Harry Styles _____.

3. I'm really _____ on tennis and I've been to Wimbledon a few times.

4. I'm not _____ of water sports. I'm scared of deep water.

5. That Netflix series is right up my _____. Joe and I are binge-watching it at the moment.

6. Going to the theatre is not my cup of _____. The plays go on for too long – I get bored!

7. I'm really _____ rugby and I would love to see a match at Twickenham one day,

8. Ballet? No, that's not my _____, I'm afraid.

9. I have a lot of _____ for Maria. Do you like her too?

10. I can't _____ having to queue at the shops. I don't have the patience for it. I just do everything online these days.

11. My son _____ spaghetti. He won't eat anything else!

12. I'm not _____ about eating out. It's so expensive and the food is often better at home!

b. Use the words and phrases to talk about things or people you, or people you know, love or don't like.

adore	can't stand	have a lot of time for
keen on	live for	more of a ... person
not crazy about	not fond of	not my cup of tea
not my thing	really into	right up my street

1. _____
2. _____
3. _____
4. _____
5. _____
6. _____
7. _____
8. _____
9. _____
10. _____
11. _____
12. _____

19 Interesting

fascinating

(very interesting)

*Science is **fascinating**. I don't understand how you can find it boring.*

gripping

(interesting and exciting)

*This new series is **gripping**. Why can't we watch the next episode?*

can't put it down

(when a book is interesting/exciting and you can't stop reading)

*This novel is brilliant. I **can't put it down**.*

intriguing

(interesting and mysterious)

*So nobody knows how they died? How **intriguing**.*

engrossed in

(find interesting so it holds your attention)

*I was so **engrossed in** my book that I didn't hear them come in.*

riveting

(very interesting, formal)

*No, please don't stop. Your story is **riveting**.*

20 Boring

like watching paint dry

(very boring, informal)

*I hate cricket. It's **like watching paint dry**.*

dull as ditchwater

(very boring, informal)

*This programme is **dull as ditchwater**. Can we watch something else, please?*

tedious

(boring and continuing for too long)

*My job is so **tedious**. I can't take it anymore!*

mind-numbing

(very boring)

*I just had the most **mind-numbing** conversation with Geoff. He was telling me all about trains.*

monotonous

(boring because it's repetitive)

*We have porridge every single day. It's so **monotonous**.*

uneventful

(in which nothing interesting happens)

*My weekend was **uneventful**. How was yours?*

Interesting, boring

a. Correct the mistakes in the following sentences.

1. I love this book. I can't take it down.

2. When will this documentary end? It's dull as water.

3. I hate football. Watching a match is like seeing paint dry.

4. Sorry, I was really engrossed on what I was doing. What did you say?

5. This task is mind-boring. I have to have a break or I'm going to go mad.

b. Rewrite each sentence using a single word with the opposite meaning. There is more than one possible answer.

1. My work is so monotonous.

_____

2. What a tedious lecture!

_____

c. Answer the questions.

1. What the last book you couldn't put down?
   _____

2. What, for you, is like watching paint dry?
   _____

3. Was your weekend uneventful?
   _____

4. When did you last watch a really gripping film? What was it?
   _____

5. What activity do you easily get engrossed in?
   _____

6. What subject at school did/do you find mind-numbing?
   _____

7. How do you make long journeys less monotonous for yourself?
   _____

8. What household chore do you think is the most tedious?
   _____

9. What was the last thing you found dull as ditchwater?
   _____

21 Clean

pristine

(very clean)

The beaches were **pristine**, not like the beaches here, with litter everywhere.

squeaky clean

(very clean, informal)

I love how **squeaky clean** my hair feels after using this shampoo.

spotless

(very clean)

The accommodation was **spotless**, which I hadn't necessarily expected from the reviews.

immaculate

(very clean)

You've kept this place **immaculate**. I'm impressed!

spick and span

The office always looks **spick and span**. It's a pleasure to work there.

sterile

(with no bacteria)

Make sure everything is **sterile** before the operation starts.

22 Dirty

grubby

(informal)

*His hands were so **grubby** I didn't want to shake hands with him.*

filthy

(very dirty)

*The dishes are still **filthy**! Is the dishwasher broken again?*

contaminated

(dirty or polluted)

*The lake is **contaminated** with sewage so don't swim in it, whatever you do.*

manky

(informal, dirty and unpleasant to look at)

*He was wearing a **manky** old T-shirt. He could have a bit of an effort.*

-spattered

(used with some nouns, e.g. mud-, blood-)

*You can't go to your interview in those mud-**spattered boots**! What the hell are you thinking?*

dingy

(dirty and dark, used about a place or object)

*What a horribly **dingy** hallway. I couldn't live in this place!*

Clean, dirty

a. Match each word or phrase with an opposite word or phrase. There are multiple ways of answering but just choose one opposite in each case.

1. dingy   a. sterile
2. contaminated   b. filthy
3. pristine   c. spick and span
4. spotless   d. manky
5. squeaky clean   e. mud-spattered
6. grubby   f. immaculate

b. Read each sentence. Then write sentences with the same meaning, using the words given. Add more details.

His hands are so dirty.

1. filthy _____

2. grubby _____

Their car is really clean.

3. spotless _____

4. immaculate _____

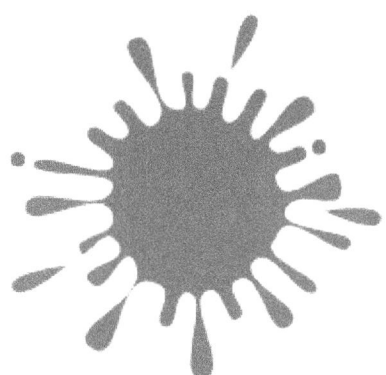

c. Complete the sentences.

1. My bedroom is _____.

2. My best friend's bedroom is _____.

3. My car is _____.

4. My nearest beach/public pool is _____.

5. The toilets at my school/university/workplace are _____.

6. The last hotel room I stayed in was _____.

7. My hands are _____

23 Have a good relationship

really get on

*Freya and I **really get on** and we have a lot in common.*

thick as thieves

(informal, get on and often talk about private things)

*You two are **thick as thieves**! What are you gossiping about this time?*

close

*They're really **close**. It's like they've known each other forever.*

get on like a house on fire

(informal)

*I didn't like him at first but now we **get on like a house on fire**.*

click

(informal, like someone instantly)

*We just **clicked** straight away and we see each other most days.*

bond

(develop a good relationship)

*The team has **bonded** well. It will make working together easier.*

24 Have a bad relationship

not get on

*I just **don't get on** with him. We're always arguing.*

can't stand

(dislike very much)

*I **can't stand** that guy! Why does he always have to be here?*

hate someone's guts

(informal, hate very much)

*I really **hate her guts**. She's always shouting at me.*

get off on the wrong foot

(immediately establish a bad relationship)

*Fred and I really **got off on the wrong foot**. Something about him really annoys me.*

not see eye to eye

(not agree with)

*I **don't see eye to eye** with my mum on most things.*

like strangers

(not interacting)

*We used to go out together but now we're **like strangers**. It's very sad.*

Have a good / bad relationship

a. Choose the correct answer for each sentence.

1. If two people get on like a house on fire, they really **like / don't like** each other.

2. If two people click, they get on **as soon as they meet / after knowing each other for a while**.

3. If you don't see eye to eye with someone, you **agree / don't agree** with them.

4. If you bond with someone, you **instantly have / develop** a good relationship with them.

5. If you can't stand someone, you dislike them **a little / a lot**.

6. If two people are like strangers, they **have never met / used to know each other**.

7. If you're thick as thieves with someone, you **tell / don't tell** them personal things.

8. If you hate someone's guts, you probably **would / wouldn't** invite them to your wedding.

9. If two people get off on the wrong foot, they dislike each other **after a period of being friends / straight away**.

10. It **is / isn't** possible to be close to someone and live far apart.

b. Complete the sentences with a person or people.

1. My brother/sister/friend can't stand _____.

2. I don't see eye to eye with _____.

3. I've always been really close to _____.

4. My mum/dad really gets/got on with _____.

5. I got off on the wrong foot with _____.

6. I used to be close to _____ but now we're like strangers.

7. _____ and I get on like a house on fire.

8. I clicked instantly with _____.

9. My best friend doesn't get on with _____ at all.

10. _____ and I are thick as thieves.

25 Close

nearby

My daughter lives **nearby**. It's nice because I get to see her very often.

a stone's throw

The cottage is only **a stone's throw** from here. You don't need the car.

just round the corner

No, it's not far. It's **just round the corner**.

within earshot

(close enough for you to hear)

Shout their names. Surely they're **within earshot**.

local

(related to your area)

The **local** school is really good. They've just got a new headmaster.

to hand

(near you and available to use)

Do you have your phone **to hand**? I left mine in the other room.

26 Far

miles away

I live **miles away**. I'm going to have to get a taxi back home.

nowhere near

The police were **nowhere near** when the accident happened.

remote

(far from people, towns etc)

She lives on a **remote** farm, with only her dogs for company.

a long way off

Don't get too excited! Easter is still **a long way off**.

from a distance

I only saw her **from a distance** but she looked as beautiful as on TV.

the outer reaches

(the most distant part of something)

They live in **the outer reaches** of Manchester.

Close, far

a. Complete the words and phrases with a meaning similar to *close*. The first letter of the words is given.

1. My l_____ park is where I go to walk my dog.

2. Wait till your sister is not within e_____ before you tell me.

3. Do you have a dictionary to h_____?

4. Come on. It won't take long to get there. It's just round the c_____.

5. The cathedral is only a s_____ throw from here.

6. Is there a pub n_____? I fancy a pint.

b. Complete the words and phrases with a meaning similar to *far*. The first letter of each word is given.

1. I wouldn't feel safe living in such a r_____ location.

2. The summer holidays are such a long w_____ off but I'm already excited.

3. To get to the o_____ reaches of the city, it's best to take a bus.

4. How could I have knocked the vase over? I was n_____ near it!

5. Ugh, the train station is m_____ away and it's raining.

6. From a d_____, it looks tiny.

c. Complete the sentences so they are true for you.

1. _____ is just round the corner from my house.

2. My local _____ is really great.

3. I've got my _____ to hand. Do you want to borrow it?

4. Only a stone's throw from my house is _____.

5. There is / isn't anyone within earshot at the moment.

6. _____ is miles away so you can't walk there.

7. My friend _____ lives on the outer reaches of _____.

8. I would / wouldn't like to live on a remote island.

9. _____ is nowhere near my house.

10. _____ is still a long way off so I don't need to plan for it yet.

27 Thirsty

parched

(very thirsty, informal)

*I'm absolutely **parched**. Please can we stop so I can buy a drink?*

dehydrated

(have not drunk enough)

*That horse is so **dehydrated** that I think it's going to die, sadly.*

gasping

(very thirsty, informal)

*I'm **gasping**. Let's have a beer!*

die of thirst

(informal)

*I'm **dying of thirst**. I haven't drunk anything all day.*

could do with

(informal)

*I **could** really **do with** a big glass of water. It's so hot.*

dry as a bone

(very thirsty, informal)

*When will they come and serve us? I'm **dry as a bone**.*

28 Hungry

could eat a horse

(very hungry, informal, funny)

I **could eat a horse**. When will they bring our food?

could murder

(very hungry, informal)

I **could murder** a burger right now!

peckish

(a little hungry, informal)

I'm a bit **peckish**. Have you got some crisps or something?

ravenous

(very hungry)

He was so **ravenous** that he ate two main courses!

starving

(very hungry)

We're all **starving**. I'll start making lunch even though it's early.

my stomach is rumbling

My stomach is rumbling. When's lunch?

Thirsty, hungry

a. Choose the correct answer according to the context.

1. I'm **parched / ravenous**. Can I have a glass of water, please?

2. The dog was **peckish / gasping** because it had been in a hot car.

3. I didn't have time for lunch so I'm **dying of thirst / starving**.

b. Rearrange the words to make sentences.

1. juice do fruit with I could a

_____

2. horse eat I a could

_____

3. rumbling stomach is my

_____

4. I a dry bone as am

_____

c. Correct the mistake in each sentence.

1. They didn't give me anything to eat in my meeting. My stomach fumbled the whole time.

2. Will you share your sandwich with me? I'm staving.

3. I'm dying of thirsty. Can you lend me a couple of pounds so I can buy a drink?

4. It's boiling hot. I couldn't do with some water.

5. He's dangerously dihydrated so we must get some fluids into him ASAP.

6. I could shoot a big bowl of pasta – it's 10pm and I haven't had dinner.

7. I'm so hungry that I could eat a cabbage.

8. If you're peckly, have a snack. I won't be making dinner for a while.

29 Expensive

cost an arm and a leg

(very expensive, informal)

*I'd love to buy that house by the beach but it **costs an arm and a leg**.*

pricey

(informal)

*£12.50? That's a bit **pricey**.*

extortionate

(too expensive)

*Mortgage rates are **extortionate** at the moment.*

overpriced

(too expensive)

*Everything in this shop is massively **overpriced**. Let's go to the shop across the road.*

rip-off

(informal, too expensive)

*£6.50 for a cup of coffee is such a **rip-off**.*

daylight robbery

(informal, too expensive)

*I'm not paying that. That's **daylight robbery!***

30 Cheap

dirt cheap

(very cheap, informal)

*These trousers are **dirt cheap**. I'm going to get two pairs.*

a steal

(informal)

*£3 for two? What **a steal**!*

cheap and cheerful

(not great quality but cheap)

*It's **cheap and cheerful** but the food is quite good.*

affordable

(cheap enough that people can buy it)

*They sell quality products at very **affordable** prices.*

bargain

(less than the usual price)

*I found a few **bargains** the other day when I was shopping. Have a look.*

won't break the bank

(informal, not too expensive)

*Come with us to the cinema. We won't eat out so it **won't break the bank**.*

Expensive, cheap

a. Put the following words and phrases in the correct column.

a steal	affordable	bargain
cheap and cheerful	cost an arm and a leg	daylight robbery
dirt cheap	extortionate	overpriced
pricey	rip-off	won't break the bank

Expensive	Cheap
1.	1.
2.	2.
3.	3.
4.	4.
5.	5.
6.	6.

b. Make a sentence using a word or phrase from the last page to say whether each thing is typically expensive or cheap.

1. fast sportscars

_____

2. large houses in the city centre

_____

3. second-hand books

_____

4. designer clothes

_____

5. taxis

_____

6. going on the underground

_____

7. tap water

_____

8. having your hair coloured, cut and blow-dried in a salon

_____

9. travelling off peak

_____

10. five-star hotels

_____

31 Eat

nibble

(bite little bits, gently)

*The mouse **nibbled** at the biscuit.*

scoff

(informal, eat fast and greedily)

*I was so hungry that I **scoffed** all of it!*

savour

(eat slowly and really enjoy it)

*I **savoured** every mouthful of that. It was delicious.*

hoover up

(informal, eat quickly and greedily)

*They're **hoovering up** the snacks. I'll have to bring more.*

polish off

(informal, finish eating quickly)

*I gave him some ice-cream and he **polished** it all **off** in five seconds.*

consume

(formal, can be used for drinks too)

*Please don't **consume** food at your desk.*

Eat

a. Complete the sentences with the correct words from the box.

| consuming | hoovering | nibbling |
| polished | savoured | scoffing |

1. Look at her _____ that cake. I guess she's not that hungry, after all.

2. Goodness, you're really _____ up your food. Don't they feed you at home?

3. I _____ off my lunch in five seconds flat. I was starving.

4. Stop _____ your burger. It makes you look greedy.

5. He didn't rush it – he really _____ his food.

6. _____ food on the premises is against company rules.

b. Answer the questions.

1. Think of three places where you mustn't consume food.

_____

2. Which phrase is more informal – *hoover up* or *savour*? What does each term mean?

_____

3. Which word means *eat little bits of something gently* – *scoff* or *nibble*? What does the other word mean?

_____

32 Speak

rabbit on

(informal, talk a lot)

*Will you stop **rabbiting on**? Maybe the others want to say something!*

mumble

(speak unclearly)

*You're **mumbling**. I can't understand a word.*

be like

(informal)

*I **was like**, "Stop that," and she **was like**, "Why should I?"*

scream

(shout)

*He **screamed** at me because he was so angry.*

snap

(say in a short, aggressive way)

*"Why not?" she **snapped**.*

whinge

(complain)

*You're always **whingeing**. Try to look on the bright side for a change.*

Speak

a. Rearrange the letters to make the correct words. Cover the previous page!

1. umbelm

2. anps

3. hewign

4. beeikl

5. bbaitnor

6. amsrce

b. Tick ✓ the correct sentence.

1. Which sentence would you say if someone is talking a lot?

She's rabbiting on again.

She's mumbling again.

2. Which sentence shows that someone is speaking too loudly?

Why are you screaming at me?

Why are you snapping at me?

3. Which sentence means that someone is complaining?

She was like, "I know!"

She whinged at me, "I know!"

33 Wait

hang on

(informal)

Hang on *a sec'. I can't find my shoes.*

hold your horses

(informal, funny)

Hold your horses*! Listen to what I have to say before you get angry.*

all in good time

(it will happen at the appropriate time)

*You'll find a boyfriend, I'm sure. **All in good time**.*

just a moment

*I'll check if there's a table free. **Just a moment**.*

hold tight

(informal, wait and don't do anything)

*I'll be back in a minute. **Hold tight** till I get back.*

bear with me

(formal)

*Please **bear with me** while I find your details.*

Wait

a. Complete each gap with the appropriate word.

1. Just a _____. I'll need to go and check that.

2. Hold _____ while I go and ask her.

3. Hold your _____, will you?

4. _____ with me and I'll find out for you. Please stay on the line.

5. _____ on. I'll get my coat and bag and be right with you.

6. The right job will come along one day. Have faith. All in _____ time.

b. Rewrite each sentence with a different phrase meaning *wait*. Different answers are possible but choose a phrase with an appropriate level of formality.

1. **Wait**. I can't do it that quickly!

_____

2. **Wait**, madam. I'll consult my manager and get back to you.

_____

3. Oh for goodness sake, **wait**! You're so impatient.

_____

4. You'll have to **wait**. It's not your turn yet.

_____

34 Look

gaze
(look for a long time, maybe while thinking of something else)
He **gazed** at the ceiling, thinking of her. He missed her so much.

glance
(give a quick, short look)
She **glanced** up from her book and saw him.

eye up
(informal, look at lustfully)
Those girls over there are **eyeing** you **up**.

stare
(look for a long time)
It's hard not to **stare** at people when they're shouting.

feast your eyes upon
(informal, funny, look at and enjoy)
Feast your eyes upon my beautiful new car.

peek
(look quickly or secretly)
I'm making your birthday cake so don't **peek**!

Look

a. Choose the correct answer.

1. She **eyed / gazed** out at the ocean, thinking of him.

2. Why are you **staring / glancing** at me like that? Do I have some food in my teeth?

3. **Feast your eyes / Peek** on this. Doesn't my new cover design look amazing?

b. Are both verbs possible in these sentences?

1. She **glanced / peeked** at it quickly.

2. He **gazed / stared** into the fire, dreamily.

3. We **feasted our eyes on / eyed up** the beautiful autumn scene.

4. She **peeked / stared** from behind the door and saw her birthday present on the table.

35 Walk

go for a stroll

(walk in a relaxed way)

*Let's go for a **stroll** around the town – it's very pretty.*

trek

(a long, difficult walk)

*We **trekked** around for hours but we couldn't find them.*

wander

(walk without purpose)

*We found her **wandering** around. I think she was lost.*

amble

(walk in a relaxed way)

*We **ambled** along the seafront. It was a lovely day.*

pace up and down

(walk with regular steps when you're nervous)

She's still **pacing up and down**. It's her wedding tomorrow and she's nervous.

tiptoe

(walk with only your toes on the ground)

She **tiptoed** down the stairs because she didn't want to wake us.

Walk

a. Replace the word *walk* or *walked* with a suitable word or phrase from the last page. More than one answer may be possible.

1. I was nervous so I **walked** up and down the corridor outside the exam hall.

_____

2. We **walked** around the town without knowing, or worrying, what our destination was.

_____

3. My sister **walked** into the room quietly because she didn't want our parents to hear her.

_____

4. We **walked** over the mountains and down the valley on the other side.

_____

5. The young couples **walked** arm in arm by the harbour at sundown.

_____

6. Tourists like to **walk** slowly along the idyllic country paths.

_____

36 Sleep

conk out

(informal, go to sleep suddenly)

*It's not surprising you **conked out**, after that long flight.*

drop off

(start to sleep)

*I **dropped off** in front of the TV last night.*

out like a light

(informal, go to sleep very quickly)

*I went **out like a light**. I must have been more tired than I thought.*

power nap

(a short sleep during the day)

*Don't make too much noise. Ethan's having a **power nap**.*

forty winks

(informal, a short sleep)

*I'm going to grab **forty winks**. See you in an hour or so.*

off to bed

(go to your bedroom to sleep)

*I'm **off to bed**. I've got an early start tomorrow.*

Sleep

a. Match the parts of the phrases.

1. drop
2. forty
3. off
4. power
5. conk
6. out

a. winks
b. to bed
c. like a light
d. out
e. off
f. nap

b. Complete the phrases, then answer the questions.

1. When was the last time you had a power _____?
_____

2. Do you have an informal phrase for sleep, like *forty* _____, in your language?
_____

3. Do you tend to go out _____ at night or does it take you a long time to fall asleep?
_____

4. Do you ever drop _____ in front of the TV?
_____

37 Die

pop your clogs

(informal, funny)

Hasn't he **popped his clogs** yet? He's at least 95!

slip away

She *slipped away* in her sleep early this morning.

kick the bucket

(informal, funny)

Haven't you heard? The President **kicked the bucket** last night.

give up the ghost

(informal, funny)

When I **give up the ghost**, I want to be cremated, not buried.

go to a better place

We miss our family dog but he's **gone to a better place**.

pass away

(a little formal)

When did you mother **pass away**?

Die

a. Which of these phrases are informal and funny? And which are neutral or a little formal?

	Informal	Neutral / Formal

1. give up the ghost

2. go to a better place

3. kick the bucket

4. pass away

5. pop your clogs

6. slip away

b. Answer the questions.

1. Which phrase is your favourite? _____

2. Are any of the phrases similar to ones in your language?
_____

3. Which phrases could you use when you're talking to someone about the death of their mother?
_____

4. Research the origins of one or more of the funny phrases.

38 Surprised

speechless

*He proposed last night. I was **speechless**!*

can't believe your eyes/ears

*I thought he'd moved to Spain but there he was. **I couldn't believe my eyes**!*

out of the blue

(without warning)

*I got a message from her, completely **out of the blue**.*

where did that come from?

(informal)

*You want to leave me? **Where did that come from?** I said you were in love.*

astonished

(a little formal)

*I'm **astonished** that you think you can treat me like this.*

taken aback

(formal)

*I was rather **taken aback** by her brutal honesty.*

Surprised

a. Complete the sentences with a suitable word or phrase. More than one answer may be possible.

1. I was _____

2. The message came completely _____

3. I couldn't _____

4. Where _____?

b. Use each of the words and phrases from the previous page in a sentence of your own.

1. _____
2. _____
3. _____
4. _____
5. _____
6. _____

39 Tired

knackered

(very tired, informal)

You wouldn't believe how **knackered** I am. I need to sit down.

worn out

You look **worn out**. Take a break!

dead on your feet

(very tired, informal)

I'm **dead on my feet** after my 12-hour night shift.

run out of steam

Jacob looks like he's **run out of steam** – shall we take him home?

your bed is calling you

(informal, funny, want to sleep)

I'd love to join you at the pub but **my bed is calling me**.

can barely keep your eyes open

(very tired, want to sleep)

We went to the cinema last night but it was a waste of money because **I could barely keep my eyes open**.

Tired

a. Complete the words and phrases. The first letter is given.

1. I can barely k_____ my e_____ open. It was a late night last night at the shop.

2. My bed is c_____ me so I'll see you tomorrow.

3. I've r_____ out of s_____. I want to go home.

4. He was d_____ on his f_____ so he didn't stay long.

5. I'm completely w_____ out. I need a holiday!

6. Are you as k_____ as you look? Sit down for a while.

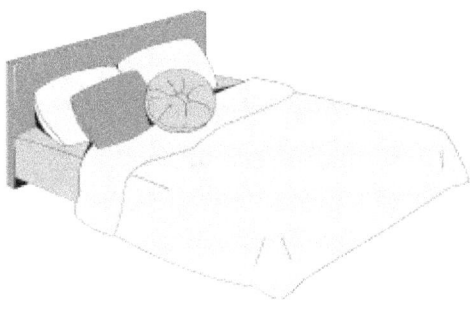

40 Lucky

blessed

*I've got a caring family and a job I love. I feel really **blessed**.*

jammy

(informal, often used when someone made no effort)

*He's so **jammy** for getting that job. I'm a bit jealous, if I'm honest.*

fluke

(good luck, which you don't think will be repeated)

*You've never played tennis before. You won but it was just a **fluke**!*

stroke of luck

*What a **stroke of luck**! They contacted you just at the right time.*

your lucky day

*It's **your lucky day**! You've won the grand prize.*

fortunate

(formal)

*I feel very **fortunate** for all that I have and I'm truly grateful.*

Lucky

a. Answer the questions.

1. "It's my lucky day!" When did you last feel like this?
___

2. What makes you feel fortunate?
___

3. When did you last have a stroke of luck? What happened?
___

4. Have you ever thought you were good at something but it was just a fluke?
___

5. Do you know someone who is often jammy?
___

6. Do you feel blessed? What makes you feel that way?
___

41　Funny

hilarious

(very funny)

The lyrics are absolutely **hilarious**. You should listen to them again.

priceless

(informal)

Sara, you really are **priceless**!

witty

(funny in a clever way)

He's very **witty**. He makes me laugh so much.

crack you up

(laugh hard at something funny)

She's always making jokes. She **cracks me up**.

hysterical

(very funny)

That is **hysterical**. You should tell the others.

amusing

(formal)

I don't find this **amusing** in the slightest. You shouldn't play practical jokes.

Funny

a. Answer the questions.

1. Which word is more formal – *amusing* or *priceless*?

2. Which word would you be more likely to use for clever humour – *hilarious* or *witty*?

3. If someone cracks you up, is this a good or a bad thing?

b. Complete the sentences to reflect your opinions and experiences.

1. The series / film _____ is hilarious.

2. The wittiest person I know is _____.

3. _____ always cracks me up.

4. I find _____ hysterical.

42 Busy

rushed off your feet

(very busy, informal)

She's been **rushed off her feet** all day so she needs a rest.

snowed under

(informal, too much to do)

I'm really **snowed under** at work. Can we meet next week instead?

in the middle of

(busy doing something)

We're **in the middle of** dinner. Can I call you back?

a lot on your plate

(informal)

I've got **a lot on my plate** right now. This is not a good time, sorry.

swamped

(informal, too much to do)

She's **swamped** so she told me she can't help me.

your hands full

He's got **his hands full** looking after the kids so we can't disturb him.

Busy

a. Rearrange the words in the large letters.

1. I can't talk now. I'm in the middle of something.

2. I've got a lot on my plate this week. Can we please postpone the meeting?

3. You must be swamped. I'll come back another time.

4. I can see your hands are full. I won't bother you.

5. He's really snowed under but that's no excuse for shouting at me!

6. Leave me alone! I'm rushed off my feet.

43 Job

calling

(a job you have a strong feeling about, especially if it's morally good)

*Being a teacher to disadvantaged kids is my **calling**.*

for a living

*What does she do **for a living**? She must earn quite a lot as both their kids go to private school.*

vocation

(a job you feel is your purpose in life)

*He loves being a doctor. It's his **vocation**.*

9–5

(a normal job, especially an office job)

*I'm tired of the **9–5**. I want a new career.*

career

(a job or series of related jobs)

*She's just begun a **career** as a photographer.*

position

(a little formal)

*There are lots of management **positions** within the company.*

Job

a. Answer the questions.

1. What do/did your parents do for a living?
___

2. Do you have a 9–5 job?
___

3. Does your best friend have a satisfying career?
___

4. Where do you look for a new position – on a website or at an recruitment agency etc?
___

5. Is your job your vocation?
___

6. Do you know someone whose job is their calling?
___

44 A lot

truckloads

(informal)

She's made **truckloads** of money from her investments.

loads

(informal)

I've got **loads** of time so there's no rush.

stacks

(informal)

If you don't like these dresses, there are **stacks** more out the back.

millions

(informal)

I've asked him **millions** of times but he still hasn't done it.

great deal

(formal)

She's got a **great deal** of knowledge on the subject so ask her.

considerable

(formal)

You've made **considerable** progress. Well done.

A lot

a. Rewrite each sentence with a different phrase meaning *a lot/lots*. Different answers are possible.

1. Don't worry, I've got **lots of** time.

_____

2. She makes **a lot of** money.

_____

3. You have **a lot of** knowledge on this subject, professor.

_____

4. The gang left **a lot of** evidence at the scene so it is believed that the police have a strong case.

_____

5. I've got **lots of** work to finish before I can go home.

_____

6. I've told you **lots of** times, I don't know.

_____

45 Important

momentous

(usually used with the words *occasion, event, decision*)

*This is a **momentous** decision so we mustn't rush it.*

be all and end all

(informal, most important thing, often used in the negative)

*Stop stressing about work. It's not the **be all and end all**.*

critical

(very important)

*It's **critical** that we ask their permission or they won't be happy.*

above all

(most importantly)

***Above all**, good friends shouldn't criticise each other. We should be supportive.*

significant

*There have been some **significant** changes since you were here last.*

crucial

(very important)

*It is **crucial** that we examine the sample carefully.*

Important

a. Correct the mistake in each sentence. Remember to cover the vocabulary on the last page!

1. Above it, you must learn to behave properly.

2. It is criticial that you tidy your desks before the director comes round.

3. Finding a man is not the be all and finish all, you know.

4. This is a truly mamentous occasion.

5. He's one of the most significent musicians of the last century.

6. Peterson played a crushial role in the match.

46 Hello

hi

(informal)

__Hi__, guys. Thanks for waiting.

hiya

(informal)

__Hiya__. Did you have a good weekend?

y'alright?

(informal, sometimes a greeting, sometimes a question, = *Are you alright?*)

__Y'alright__, Max. What have you got planned for today?

morning

(informal)

__Morning__, everyone. Let's go in – they're expecting us.

hello there

(used when calling for someone)

__Hello there__! Can you hear me?

good morning, good afternoon, good evening

(formal)

__Good afternoon__, sir. The meeting is currently underway in Room 23, if you'd care to join them.

Hello

a. Choose the best word or phrase for each situation. There may be more than one possible answer.

1. Which would you use to greet your boss? Your answer will depend on how formal your workplace is and on your relationship with your boss.
   _____

2. Which would you use to greet your teacher at school?
   _____

3. How would you greet your friends in English?
   _____

4. Which would you use for calling to someone from far away?
   _____

5. Which would you use with a hotel receptionist?
   _____

6. How would you greet your mum or dad in English?
   _____

7. How would you greet someone formally at 12 noon?
   _____

47 Bye

see you later

*It's been lovely chatting to you. **See you later**.*

bye-bye

*I hope you enjoyed yourself. **Bye-bye** for now.*

catch you later

(informal)

*It was so good to see you. **Catch you later**.*

take care

*We mustn't leave it so long next time. **Take care**!*

goodbye

(formal)

***Goodbye** and see you at the next meeting, I hope.*

have a nice day

(formal, used to a customer in a shop, etc)

*Here is your coffee. **Have a nice day**.*

Bye

a. Match the two parts of each word or phrase, without looking at the previous page.

1. catch   a. you later

2. good   b. a nice day

3. have   c. bye

4. bye-   d. you later

5. see   e. care

6. take   f. bye

b. Which are formal? Name some situations in which you use these formal greetings.

_____

_____

_____

48 Thank you

ta

(informal)

Ta, Joe. I couldn't have done it without you.

many thanks

Many thanks for my leaving present. I was really touched.

you're a life saver

(informal)

*Thanks for looking after the kids while I was working. **You're a life saver.***

can't thank you enough

*What you did was so thoughtful. **I can't thank you enough.***

you shouldn't have

(used when you get a present)

*The flowers are beautiful. **You shouldn't have!***

much appreciated

(a little formal)

*Oh, did you finish the report for me? **Much appreciated.***

Thank you

a. Complete the phrases.

1. many _____

2. much _____

3. you _____ have

4. you're a life _____

5. I can't thank you _____

b. Think of four situations where someone has done something kind for you recently. Use four different phrases to thank the people.

1. _____

2. _____

3. _____

4. _____

49 I'm sorry

I hope you can forgive me

I hope you can forgive me for forgetting your birthday. I've been so busy.

my bad

(informal)

Oh no, my bad! I gave you the wrong answer.

I owe you an apology

I owe you an apology. I forgot to send the email you asked me to.

excuse me

(formal)

Excuse me for interrupting you. Please carry on.

ever so sorry

(formal)

I'm ever so sorry for breaking the vase. I'll buy you a new one.

my apologies

(formal)

I didn't mean to be rude. My apologies.

I'm sorry

a. Add an extra sentence apologising for each situation.

1. I crashed your car. _____

2. Oh, I interrupted you! _____

3. I'm going to be late for the meeting. _____

4. I ran over your cat. _____

5. I've spilled your drink, mate. _____

b. What have you done recently that you've been sorry for? Now you know these phrases, which would you use for that situation?

_____

50 I think

from where I'm standing

(informal)

From where I'm standing, she really has no choice.

I reckon

(informal)

I reckon it's about half past two now.

as far as I'm concerned

As far as I'm concerned, this is a ridiculous idea.

the way I see it

(informal)

The way I see it, she should not go with him to the party.

if you ask me

(informal)

If you ask me, he's completely wrong.

it is my view

(formal)

It is my view that we cannot be too careful about this.

I think

a. Rearrange the words to make phrases. Don't look at the last page.

1. where from standing I'm _____

2. reckon I _____

3. as concerned as I'm far _____

4. way see the it I _____

5. you if me ask _____

6. view it my is _____

b. Give your opinion on the following things, using the phrases above.

1. the best film in the world

_____

2. the most gorgeous man/woman in the world

_____

3. the best country to live in

_____

4. the best way to improve your local area

_____

5. which is more useful – a washing machine or a hoover

_____

Answers

Units 1, 2   Very good, very bad

a.

Very good	Very bad
1. amazing	1. awful
2. brilliant	2. horrendous
3. first-rate	3. not up to scratch
4. in a class of its own	4. second-rate
5. outstanding	5. terrible
6. something else	6. the pits

b.
1. amazing
2. first-rate
3. the pits
4. not up to scratch
5. horrendous
6. in a class of his own
7. outstanding
8. terrible
9. awful
10. second-rate

Units 3, 4   Very big, very small

a.

	Very big	Very small
1. miniscule		✓
2. fit in the palm of your hand		✓
3. whopping great	✓	
4. massive	✓	
5. tiny		✓
6. huge	✓	
7. as big as a house	✓	
8. microscopic		✓
9. gigantic	✓	
10. invisible to the naked eye		✓
11. minute		✓
12. immense	✓	

b.
1. massive / huge / gigantic / immense
2. miniscule / tiny / microscopic / minute
3. whopping great / massive / huge / gigantic / immense
4. miniscule / tiny / microscopic / invisible to the naked eye / minute
5. miniscule / tiny / microscopic / minute
6. massive / huge / as big as a house / gigantic / immense
7. miniscule / tiny / microscopic / invisible to the naked eye / minute

Units 5, 6   Attractive, ugly

a.
1. easy on the eye
2. exquisite
3. hot
4. drop-dead gorgeous
5. fanciable / fit
6. fanciable / fit

b.
1. not much to look at
2. unprepossessing / unsightly
3. unprepossessing / unsightly
4. no oil painting
5. minger
6. hideous

c.
Your own answers

d.
Your own answers

Units 7, 8   Easy, difficult

a.
1. sleep
2. park
3. rocket
4. piece
5. breeze
6. foolproof

b.
1. arduous
2. taxing
3. picnic

4. pressed
5. tricky
6. demanding

c.
Your own answers

Units 9, 10 Happy, sad

a.
1. f
2. e
3. b
4. c
5. a
6. d

b.
Happy = smile from ear to ear, over the moon, jump for joy
Sad = grief-stricken, reduced to tears, cut up

c.
(in any order)
1. down
2. depressed
3. downcast

d.
1. thrilled
2. glad
3. chuffed

e.
Your own answers

Units 11, 12 Heavy, light

a.

Heavy	Light
1. dead weight	1. insubstantial
2. hefty	2. light as a feather
3. laden	3. lightweight
4. top-heavy	4. not weigh a thing
5. weigh a tonne	5. portable
6. weighty	6. weigh nothing

b.
1. as light as a feather
2. insubstantial
3. a tonne
4. laden
5. a dead weight

Units 13, 14 Dark, bright

a.
1. glaring / gleaming
2. glaring / gleaming
3. dazzling

b.
1. Day
2. dimly
3. ablaze
4. thing

c.
Your own answers

Units 15   Intelligent, stupid

a.
1. noun
2. noun
3. adjective
4. adjective
5. adjective

b.
1. You have to admit, she's not just a pretty face.
2. You have to admit, she's (very) bright.
3. You have to admit, she's a (real / right) brainbox.
4. You have to admit, she's a (real) bright spark.

c. and d.
Your own answers

Units 17, 18 I love, I don't like

a.
1. live
2. person
3. keen
4. fond
5. street
6. tea
7. into
8. thing
9. time
10. stand
11. adores
12. crazy

b.
Your own answers

Units 19, 20 Interesting, boring

a.
1. I love this book. I can't **put** it down.
2. When will this documentary end? It's dull as **ditchwater**.
3. I hate football. Watching a match is like **watching** paint dry.
4. Sorry, I was really engrossed **in** what I was doing. What did you say?
5. This task is mind-**numbing**. I have to have a break or I'm going to go mad.

b.
1. My work is so fascinating / gripping / intriguing / riveting.
2. What a fascinating / gripping / intriguing / riveting lecture!

c.
Your own answers

Units 21, 22 Clean, dirty

a.
1. a / c / f
2. a / c / f
3. b / d / e
4. b / d / e
5. b / d / e
6. a / c / f

b.
(with example extra details)
1. His hands are so filthy. He never washes them.
2. His hands are so grubby. Doesn't he know how to use soap?
3. Their car is (really) spotless. They have it valeted every few days!
4. Their car is (really) immaculate. Their daughter cleans it to earn pocket money.

c.
Your own answers

Units 23, 24 Have a good / bad relationship

a.
1. like
2. as soon as they meet
3. don't agree
4. develop
5. a lot
6. used to know each other
7. tell
8. wouldn't
9. straight away
10. is

b.
Your own answers

Units 25, 26 Close, far

a.
1. local
2. earshot
3. hand
4. corner
5. stone's
6. nearby

b.
1. remote
2. way
3. outer
4. nowhere
5. miles
6. distance

c.
Your own answers

Units 27, 28 Thirsty, hungry

a.
1. parched
2. gasping
3. starving

b.
1. I could do with a fruit juice.
2. I could eat a horse.
3. My stomach is rumbling.
4. I am as dry as a bone.

c.
1. They didn't give me anything to eat in my meeting. My stomach **rumbled** the whole time.
2. Will you share your sandwich with me? I'm **starving**.
3. I'm dying of **thirst**. Can you lend me a couple of pounds so I can buy a drink?
4. It's boiling hot. I **could** do with some water.
5. He's dangerously **dehydrated** so we must get some fluids into him ASAP.
6. I could **murder** a big bowl of pasta – it's 10pm and I haven't had dinner.
7. I'm so hungry that I could eat a **horse**.
8. If you're **peckish**, have a snack. I won't be making dinner for a while.

Units 29, 30 Expensive, cheap

a.

Expensive	Cheap
1. cost an arm and a leg	1. a steal
2. daylight robbery	2. affordable
3. extortionate	3. bargain
4. overpriced	4. cheap and cheerful
5. pricey	5. dirt cheap
6. rip-off	6. won't break the bank

b.
(example answers – your answers may vary)
1. Fast sportscars cost an arm and a leg / are daylight robbery / are extortionate / are overpriced / are pricey / are a rip-off.
2. Large houses in the city centre cost an arm and a leg / are daylight robbery / are extortionate / are overpriced / are pricey / are a rip-off.
3. Second-hand books are a steal / are affordable / are a bargain / are cheap and cheerful / are dirt cheap / won't break the bank.
4. Designer clothes cost an arm and a leg / are daylight robbery / are extortionate / are overpriced / are pricey / are a rip-off.
5. Taxis cost an arm and a leg / are daylight robbery / are extortionate / are overpriced / are pricey / are a rip-off.

6. Going on the underground is affordable / is a bargain / is dirt cheap / won't break the bank.
7. Tap water is a steal / is affordable / is a bargain / is cheap and cheerful / is dirt cheap / won't break the bank.
8. Having your hair coloured, cut and blow-dried in a salon costs an arm and a leg / is daylight robbery / is extortionate / is overpriced / is pricey / is a rip-off.
9. Travelling off peak is a steal / is affordable / is a bargain / is cheap and cheerful / is dirt cheap / won't break the bank.
10. Five-star hotels cost an arm and a leg / are daylight robbery / are extortionate / are overpriced / are pricey / are a rip-off.

Unit 31   Eat

a.
1. nibbling
2. hoovering
3. polished
4. scoffing
5. savoured
6. Consuming

b.
1. (example answer) in a museum, in a lesson, in a swimming pool!
2. *Hoover up* is more informal. Hoover up = eat quickly and greedily. Savour = eat slowly and really enjoy it.
3. *Nibble* means eat little bits of something gently. Scoff = eat fast and greedily.

Unit 32   Speak

a.
1. mumble
2. snap
3. whinge
4. be like
5. rabbit on
6. scream

b.
1. She's rabbiting on again.
2. Why are you screaming at me?
3. She whinged at me, "I know!"

Unit 33   Wait

a.
1. moment
2. tight
3. horses
4. Bear
5. Hang
6. good

b.
1. Hang on / Hold your horses / Just a moment. I can't do it that quickly!
2. Just a moment / Bear with me, madam. I'll consult my manager and get back to you.
3. Oh for goodness sake, hang on / hold your horses / just a moment! You're so impatient.
4. You'll have to hang on / hold tight / bear with me. It's not your turn yet.

Unit 34   Look

a.
1. gazed
2. staring
3. Feast your eyes

b.
1. yes
2. yes
3. only *feasted our eyes*
4. only *peeked*

Unit 35   Walk

a.
1. paced
2. ambled (or *went for a stroll / wandered*)
3. tiptoed
4. trekked
5. went for a stroll (or *ambled / wandered*)
6. amble / wander

Unit 36   Sleep

a.
1. e
2. a

116

3. b
4. f
5. d
6. c

b.
1. nap
2. winks
3. like a light
4. off

Unit 37   Die

a.

	Informal	Neutral/Formal
1. give up the ghost	✓	
2. go to a better place		✓
3. kick the bucket	✓	
4. pass away		✓
5. pop your clogs	✓	
6. slip away		✓

b.
1. Your own answer
2. Your own answer
3. go to a better place / pass away / slip away
4. Your own answer

Unit 38   Surprised

a.
1. speechless / astonished / taken aback
2. out of the blue
3. believe my eyes / ears
4. did that come from

b.
Your own answers

Unit 39   Tired

a.
1. keep my eyes open
2. calling
3. run out of steam
4. dead on his feet
5. worn out
6. knackered

Unit 40   Lucky

a.
Your own answers

Unit 41   Funny

a.
1. amusing
2. witty
3. a good thing

b.
Your own answers

Unit 42   Busy

a.
1. middle
2. plate
3. swamped
4. hands
5. snowed
6. rushed

Unit 43   Job

a.
Your own answers

Unit 44   A lot

a.
1. Don't worry, I've got truckloads of / loads of / stacks of time.
2. She makes truckloads of / loads of / stacks of / a great deal of money.
3. You have a great deal of / considerable knowledge on this subject, professor.
4. The gang left a great deal of / (a) considerable (amount of) evidence at the scene so it is believed that the police have a strong case.
5. I've got truckloads of / loads of / stacks of / a great deal of / a considerable amount of work to finish before I can go home.
6. I've told you truckloads of / loads of / stacks of / millions of times, I don't know.

Unit 45   Important

a.
1. Above **all**, you must learn to behave properly.
2. It is **critical** that you tidy your desks before the director comes round.
3. Finding a man is not the be all and **end** all, you know.
4. This is a truly **momentous** occasion.
5. He's one of the most **significant** musicians of the last century.
6. Peterson played a **crucial** role in the match.

Unit 46   Hello

a.
1. Informal: Hi / Hiya / Y'alright? / Morning. Formal: Good morning.
2. Good morning.
3. Hi / Hiya / Y'alright? / Morning.
4. Hello there.
5. Good morning / Good afternoon / Good evening.
6. Informal: Hi / Hiya / Y'alright? / Morning. Formal: Good morning / Good afternoon / Good evening.
7. Good afternoon.

Unit 47   Bye

a.
1. d
2. c
3. b
4. a
5. e

b.
Formal: goodbye, have a nice day
Goodbye: (examples) at a formal meeting, at the end of a formal telephone

conversation

Have a nice day: (examples) at the end of a formal telephone conversation, to a customer in a shop

Unit 48   Thank you

a.
1. thanks
2. appreciated
3. shouldn't
4. saver
5. enough

b.
Your own answers

Unit 49   I'm sorry

a.
1. I hope you can forgive me / I owe you an apology / I'm ever so sorry / My apologies.
2. My bad / Excuse me / I'm ever so sorry / My apologies.
3. I hope you can forgive me / Excuse me / I'm ever so sorry / My apologies.
4. I hope you can forgive me / I owe you an apology / I'm ever so sorry / My apologies.
5. I hope you can forgive me / My bad / I owe you an apology.

b.
Your own answers

Unit 50   I think

a.
1. from where I'm standing
2. I reckon
3. as far as I'm concerned
4. the way I see it
5. if you ask me
6. it is my view

b.
Your own answers

DID YOU ENJOY THIS BOOK?
Please leave me a review. Thank you.

★★★★★

WOULD YOU LIKE THIS FREE STORY, ADAPTED BY ME FOR LEARNERS OF ENGLISH?

I also write graded readers, which are stories that are adapted to your level of English. To get a free graded reader story, visit my website and enter your email address. You will also get news about my new books.

www.ReadStories-LearnEnglish.com

Why read graded readers?

- The stories are in modern English, and they have grammar & vocabulary **at your level**.
- There are **definitions** of difficult words.
- Studies show that learners who read in English **improve in all areas much more quickly** than learners who don't read.
- You can improve your English **without extra studying** and with **very little effort**.
- Reading stories is the **best way to learn vocabulary and grammar** in context. You will **learn a lot without realising** it!

www.ingramcontent.com/pod-product-compliance
Lightning Source LLC
Chambersburg PA
CBHW081620100526
44590CB00021B/3529